# $\mathscr{A}$DVENT *and*
# $\mathscr{C}$HRISTMAS
# $\mathscr{W}$ISDOM
## —— *from* ——
## SAINT BENEDICT

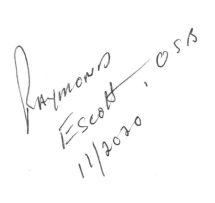

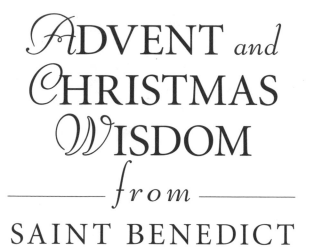

# ADVENT and CHRISTMAS WISDOM
## from
## SAINT BENEDICT

Daily Scripture and Prayers Together
With Saint Benedict's Own Words

Compiled by Judith Sutera, OSB

Liguori
LIGUORI, MISSOURI

Imprimi Potest: Thomas D. Picton, C.Ss.R.
Provincial, Denver Province, The Redemptorists

Published by Liguori Publications, Liguori, Missouri
www.liguori.org

**Library of Congress Cataloging-in-Publication Data**

Advent and Christmas wisdom from Saint Benedict: daily scripture and prayers together with Saint Benedict's own words / compilation, prayers, and actions by Judith Sutera.
    p. cm.
    ISBN 978-0-7648-1883-7
    1. Advent—Prayers and devotions. 2. Christmas—Prayers and devotions. 3. Bible—Quotations. 4. Benedict, Saint, Abbot of Monte Cassino.—Quotations. I. Sutera, Judith. II. Benedict, Saint, Abbot of Monte Cassino. Selections. English.
    BV40.A37 2010
    242'.2—dc22

                                 2010020303

Printed in the United States of America
14 13 12 11 10   5 4 3 2 1
First Edition

# Contents

# Introduction

Many who read the *Rule of St. Benedict* for the first time find themselves rather disappointed. There is little in the way of poetic reflection or spiritual treatise. In fact, the casual reader is justified in asking, "Is that all there is to it? What are people seeing here that makes it so enduring or endearing?" Much of it is simply a stringing together of earlier sources, and especially passages of Scripture. The rest seems to be practical advice and basic organizational principles for such things as praying the Divine Office and serving meals.

Indeed, what has made this little *Rule* so important to religious communities and, in fact, many institutions of Western civilization is the very fact that it does *not* preach esoteric spiritual disciplines. Benedict recognizes the great core truth that most of our earthly existence does not occur in ecstatic moments of divine enlightenment, but in the ordinary moments of daily life. If we can be aware of the presence of God in each of these moments and do each small thing with holy attentiveness, then we will be able to attain great insight for the whole of life. The transformation toward a deeper relationship with God proceeds from the self-awareness that comes with doing each act as if it matters. Every moment is part of the journey, and everything happens in the sight of God.

Benedict wrote his rule at the end of a period of great spiritual exploration. Institutional religious life had been evolving as an amalgam of the best practices of early Christian communal life. Its ideal comprised the Jerusalem community described in the Acts of the Apostles, the contemplative quest of the Greek philosophers, and the post-persecution desire for a life of sacrifice and God-centered living as exemplified in the stories of the desert fathers and mothers. There were numerous ascetic communities and numerous rules for their ways of life. Little in the *Rule of St. Benedict* is original; rather, it is a synthesis of all the essential elements expressed and lived in the first five centuries of Christianity, with some masterful editing and focusing.

Benedict and his sister Scholastica, who has traditionally been identified as his twin, were born in Italy in 480. A rule for monasteries attributed to him has been in use for over 1500 years, but nowhere does the author identify himself or provide any biographical or personal information. The only other source is a biography written in the 590s, around 50 years after Benedict's death, which claims to use contemporary accounts and eyewitness reports. It is Book II of a group of four dialogues on holy persons attributed to Pope St. Gregory the Great. Since the two documents and the tradition were handed down in association with one another, it is generally assumed that the man in the biography and the author of the rule were the same person, but there is no solid internal evidence.

This, of course, makes it a little more difficult to produce a book of meditations like this one. St. Benedict gives instructions for the mechanics of liturgical prayer, but never writes any reflections about or for the liturgical year. There are no homilies or scriptural exegetical writings. There is little self-expression—nothing that suggests his own spiritual journey or theology—except what can be extrapolated from his rule. There is only his vision of how a harmonious community of Christians would live and how each person in it might find knowledge of self and God.

This book, then, must take a similar approach. In Advent, as always, Christians must struggle to see God in the mundane, to understand the unity of all creation, to maintain a mindfulness that makes all life a prayer.

This book uses an adapted version of the translation of *The Rule of St. Benedict* by Father Boniface Verheyen, OSB, copyright 1949, with permission of St. Benedict's Abbey in Atchison, Kansas.

Texts from the *Dialogues of St. Gregory* are the author's own versions of the Latin text.

# How to Use This Book

ADVENT—that period of great anticipatory joy—is a time of preparation for the celebration of Jesus' arrival in Bethlehem as a helpless infant. In the Western liturgy, Advent begins four Sundays prior to December 25—the Sunday closest to November 30, which is the feast of Saint Andrew, Jesus' first disciple.

The annual commemoration of Jesus' birth begins the Christmas cycle of the liturgical year—a cycle that runs from Christmas Eve to the Sunday after the feast of the Epiphany. In keeping with the unfolding of the message of the liturgical year, this book is designed to be used during the entire period from the First Sunday of Advent to the end of the Christmas cycle.

The four weeks of Advent are often thought of as symbolizing the four ways Jesus comes into the world: (1) at his birth as a helpless infant at Bethlehem, (2) at his arrival in the hearts of believers, (3) at his death, and (4) at his arrival on Judgment Day.

Because Christmas falls on a different day of the week each year, the fourth week of Advent is never really finished; it is abruptly, joyously, and solemnly abrogated by the annual coming again of Jesus at Christmas. Christ's Second Coming will also one day abruptly interrupt our sojourn here on earth.

Since the calendar dictates the number of days in Advent, this book includes Scripture and meditation readings for a full twenty-eight days. These twenty-eight daily readings make up Part I of this book. It is suggested the reader begin at the beginning and on Christmas switch to Part II, which contains materials for the twelve days of Christmas. "Extra" entries from Part I may be read by doubling up days or by reading two entries on weekends. Alternately, one may just skip the entries that do not fit within the Advent time frame for that particular year.

Each "day" in this book begins with the words of St. Benedict taken from sources acknowledged on pages 113 and 114. Following the quotation is a Scripture excerpt related in some way to the beginning quote. Next is a small prayer also built on the ideas from the two preceding passages. Finally, an Advent or Christmas activity is suggested as a way to apply the messages to one's daily life.

Part III proposes two optional formats for using each day as part of a longer liturgical observance similar to Night Prayer combined with a version of the Office of Readings. These options are for those who may wish to use this book as part of a more developed individual or group observance. The purpose of these readings is to enrich the Advent/Christmas/Epiphany season of the liturgical year and set up a means by which individuals, families, or groups can observe the true meaning of the season.

## PART I

~~~~~~~

# READINGS *for* ADVENT

## Longing for Life

The Lord, seeking his laborer in the multitude to whom He proclaims these words, says again, "Who is the one who desires life, and loves to see good days?"

*RULE OF ST. BENEDICT, PROLOGUE: SECTION 14*

### SCRIPTURE

*Therefore, thus says the LORD, I have returned to Jerusalem with compassion; my house shall be built in it, says the LORD of hosts, and the measuring line shall be stretched out over Jerusalem. Proclaim further: Thus says the LORD of hosts: My cities shall again overflow with prosperity; the LORD will again comfort Zion and again choose Jerusalem.*

ZECHARIAH 1:16–18

## PRAYER

Giver of all gifts, you have made many promises to those who love you. As I await the birthday of your greatest promise, your own Son, help me to see the many ways in which he comes into our world and the many ways in which I can find him today. Open my eyes and my heart to the graces of this Advent season so that I may prosper in goodness and holiness.

## ADVENT ACTION

Advent commemorates the coming of Jesus as a human being into the world. Yet this was not a one-day-in-history event. Jesus is born again in every moment if believers have the eyes to see him in others, the ears to hear his teachings in daily events, the hearts to be in conversation with him in prayer. Advent serves as a reminder to pay attention. Stop momentarily throughout the day and say to God, "Here I am. I am one who longs for life." Remember that the prosperity promised here is not about financial riches or personal glory, but the well being that comes from faith, hope, and love. Look around at the signs of your own "wealth," and thank God for the divine presence in your life.

## Pick Me

*I*f, hearing this, you answer, "I am the one," God says to you, "If you will have true and everlasting life, keep your tongue from evil and your lips from speaking guile; turn away from evil and do good; seek after peace and pursue it. And when you shall have done these things, my eyes shall be upon you and my ears unto your prayers And before you shall call upon Me, I will say, 'Behold, I am here.'"

*RULE OF ST. BENEDICT*, PROLOGUE: 16–18

### SCRIPTURE

*But you, Israel, my servant, Jacob, whom I have chosen, the offspring of Abraham, my friend; you whom I took from the ends of the earth, and called from its farthest corners, saying to you, "You are my servant, I have chosen you and not cast you off"; do not fear, for I am with you, do not be afraid, for I am your God; I will strengthen you, I will help you, I will uphold you with my victorious right hand.*

ISAIAH 41:8–10

## PRAYER

Ever-present God, I am one who longs for life. Although I am sometimes slow to answer, I believe in your presence and your desire to bless me. Help me in this Advent season to remember that you are here in all that I do and all who I encounter.

## ADVENT ACTION

The prologue of the rule centers on a beautiful conversation between God and each human being. It is always God who starts the dialogue, calling out to each beloved creature and waiting patiently for a response. It's hard to imagine that anyone would not want happiness now and everlasting life besides. Yet there are many days when it seems an overwhelming task to follow God's simple instruction. Write out one of the passages above or another that speaks of God's faithfulness to you, and place it somewhere where you will see it each day as a reminder of God's presence.

# God's Mountain

*B*ut let us ask the Lord with the Prophet, saying to Him: "Lord, who shall dwell in Thy tabernacle [tent], or who shall rest in Thy holy mountain?"

*RULE OF ST. BENEDICT, PROLOGUE: 23*

## SCRIPTURE

*In days to come the mountain of the Lord's house shall be established as the highest of the mountains, and shall be raised above the hills; all the nations shall stream to it. Many peoples shall come and say, "Come, let us go up to the mountain of the Lord, to the house of the God of Jacob; that he may teach us his ways and that we may walk in his paths." For out of Zion shall go forth instruction, and the*

*word of the Lord from Jerusalem. He shall judge between*
*the nations, and shall arbitrate for many peoples; they shall*
*beat their swords into ploughshares, and their spears into*
*pruning-hooks; nation shall not lift up sword against nation,*
*neither shall they learn war any more. O house of Jacob,*
*come, let us walk in the light of the Lord!*

ISAIAH 2:2–5

## PRAYER

God, you have prepared a glorious home for us in heaven,
but you also wish us to establish your kingdom on earth.
Help me to move toward your kingdom this Advent by my
acts of justice. Lead me to everlasting light and help me in
my journey to your mountain of eternal life.

## ADVENT ACTION

The mountain of the Lord in the Old Testament was that
ideal place where all harmony among people would be re-
stored and all would glory in the ways of God. St. Benedict
points out in many places that we are all on the journey
to this place, but that we also can symbolically make this
place present by making our own places a reflection of it.
Advent recalls the time when the world awaited Jesus, but
it is also, right here today, a time of waiting for Jesus to
come again. The world is still torn by war and mistreat-
ment of people. Each act of peacemaking is a step toward
the holy mountain. Find a way to express this by some

.ction on behalf of world peace: learning more about an area of conflict, supporting a charity which aids victims of war, writing to a government leader expressing concerns about war, and especially, practicing non-violence in your words or actions toward others.

## DAY 4

## *Not to Us, Lord*

After this question, let us listen to the Lord answering and showing us the way, saying: "Those that walk without blemish and work justice; that speak truth in their heart; who have not used deceit in their tongue, nor done evil to a neighbor, nor taken up a reproach against a neighbor...who fearing the Lord are not puffed up by their goodness of life, but holding that the actual good which is in them cannot be done by themselves, but by the Lord, they praise the Lord working in them saying with the Prophet: 'Not to us, O Lord, not to us; but to Thy name give glory.' "

*RULE OF ST. BENEDICT*, PROLOGUE: 24–27, 29–30

*"Let the one who boasts, boast in the Lord." For it is not those who commend themselves that are approved, but those whom the Lord commends.*

2 CORINTHIANS 10:17–18

## PRAYER

Source of all goodness, you rely on us to help bring good into our world. I know that everything I am and do is a gift from you. Help me to serve others while remembering that it is you at work in me. Give me both strength and humility, and so give glory to your most holy name.

## ADVENT ACTION

Humility in the monastic tradition is not about thinking you are no good or have no talents. Goodness of life is something for which to strive. It is a blessing to have done good deeds, but the blessing is lost if we give ourselves the credit. Every good act is an opportunity to praise God. Make a list of some of your unique talents and strengths. Choose at least one way in which you will use one to be a special Christmas gift to someone this season.

# Good Deeds

*I*n the first place, beg of God by most earnest prayer, that He perfect whatever good you begin, in order that He who has been pleased to count us in the number of His children, need never be grieved at our evil deeds. For we ought at all times so to serve Him with the good things which He has given us.

RULE OF ST. BENEDICT, PROLOGUE: 4--6

## SCRIPTURE

*For the grace of God has appeared, bringing salvation to all, training us to renounce impiety and worldly passions, and in the present age to live lives that are self-controlled, upright, and godly, while we wait for the blessed hope and the manifestation of the glory of our great God and Saviour, Jesus Christ. He it is who gave himself for us that he might redeem us from all iniquity and purify for himself a people of his own who are zealous for good deeds.*

TITUS 2:11–14

## PRAYER

God, most loving parent, help me to live a good life as I await the coming of your Son Jesus. May whatever I do today begin and end in your name. Let all my efforts be made holy by your power, that you may be pleased with the humble efforts of your loving child.

## ADVENT ACTION

Advent is not merely a time to wait passively for the coming of Jesus. Jesus is reborn in every good work that is done for another, in every act that moves the world even the tiniest distance towards its fulfillment in God. Each of us is called to be a bearer of Jesus. Remember how scouts are told that they should do a good deed every day? Perhaps there was a time, as a child, when you tried to practice this, searching eagerly for something you could do. Remember how good you felt? Look for some small thing to do today that makes you feel that way again. Perhaps you'll want to feel that way again tomorrow—thus will Jesus appear once more on earth.

## Waiting

*T*herefore, our days are lengthened to a truce for the amendment of the misdeeds of our present life.... Now that we have asked the Lord who it is that shall dwell in His tent, we have heard the conditions for dwelling there; and if we fulfill the duties of tenants, we shall be heirs of the kingdom of heaven.

RULE OF ST. BENEDICT, PROLOGUE: 36, 39

SCRIPTURE

*The Lord is not slow about his promise, as some think of slowness, but is patient with you, not wanting any to perish, but all to come to repentance. But the day of the Lord will come like a thief, and then the heavens will pass away* with a loud noise, and the elements will be dissolved with fire, and the earth and everything that is done on it will be disclosed. Since all these things are to be dissolved in this way, what sort of people ought you to be in leading lives of holiness and godliness, waiting for and hastening the coming of the day of God, because of which the heavens will be set ablaze and dissolved, and the elements will melt with fire? But, in accordance with his promise, we wait for new heavens and a new earth, where righteousness is at home. Therefore, beloved, while you are waiting for these things, strive to be found by him at peace, without spot or blemish; and regard the patience of our Lord as salvation.

2 PETER 3:9–15

## PRAYER

Patient God, I await your Son who came once but is still coming. Make me ever ready to receive you, especially in those circumstances where the waiting is hard and I cannot feel your presence. Pour out your grace that I may live in holy longing, and help me bear my burdens with hope in the coming of your kingdom.

## ADVENT ACTION

We are a culture of instant gratification. We are easily tempted by the ad that promises that we can lose weight, get rich, or remove wrinkles within days, with a minimum of effort. The discipline of doing God's will is not so quick and easy. Neither is bearing with things that we have repeatedly asked God to fix. Advent is identified with waiting, and waiting is not usually a pleasant experience. Yet God waits for us so much: waits for us to do the right thing to another, to give up a sinful or detrimental practice, to turn to prayer (and not just when we want something). Think about a time when you were anxiously waiting for something or someone. Now recall the feelings of relief and happiness that followed when the waiting was over. This is the joy that signifies the coming of the new kingdom. Is someone waiting for you to do the right thing today? Is there something you need to stop waiting to do?

## DAY 7

# Make Straight the Way

*O*ur hearts and our bodies must, therefore, be ready to do battle under the biddings of holy obedience; and let us ask the Lord that He supply by the help of His grace what is impossible to us by nature. And if, flying from the pains of hell, we desire to reach life everlasting, then, while there is yet time, and we are still in the flesh, and are able during the present life to fulfill all these things, we must make haste to do now what will profit us forever.

*RULE OF ST. BENEDICT, PROLOGUE: 40–44*

## SCRIPTURE

*A voice cries out: "In the wilderness prepare the way of the Lord, make straight in the desert a highway for our God.*

*Every valley shall be lifted up, and every mountain and hill*
*be made low; the uneven ground shall become level, and the*
*rough places a plain. Then the glory of the Lord shall be re-*
*vealed, and all people shall see it together, for the mouth of*
*the Lord has spoken." A voice says, "Cry out!" And I said,*
*"What shall I cry?" All people are grass, their constancy is*
*like the flower of the field. The grass withers, the flower fades,*
*when the breath of the Lord blows upon it; surely the people*
*are grass. The grass withers, the flower fades; but the word*
*of our God will stand forever.*

ISAIAH 40:3–8

## PRAYER

Your Word made flesh, dear God, challenges me to continue the work of smoothing your way in a rugged and
damaged world. When the way is crooked and hilly, give
me the grace that is impossible by human nature alone.
Bless all those who are persecuted for defending you and
supply me the courage to be a prophetic voice crying out
in our wilderness.

## ADVENT ACTION

Prophets are those who are willing to give their hearts and
bodies to the never-ending battle with sin and injustice
in the world. We may not always be able to straighten the
way with heavy earth-moving equipment, but we can at
least remove one little rock. Do something prophetic to-

day: Write a letter to a representative about a justice issue, contribute to a social concerns organization, share with another about something you believe in, or just respond if someone is saying or doing something unjust with which you feel uncomfortable.

## Mind and Voice

We believe that God is present everywhere and that the eyes of the Lord behold the good and the bad in every place. Let us firmly believe this, especially when we take part in the Work of God. Let us, therefore, always be mindful of what the Prophet says, "Serve the Lord with fear" and again, "Sing ye wisely." And, "I will sing praise to you in the sight of the angels." Therefore, let us consider how it becomes us to behave in the sight of God and His angels, and let us so stand to sing, that our mind may be in harmony with our voice.

*RULE OF ST. BENEDICT, 19:1–7*

## SCRIPTURE

*Rejoice always, pray without ceasing, give thanks in all circumstances; for this is the will of God in Christ Jesus for you. Do not quench the Spirit. Do not despise the words of prophets, but test everything; hold fast to what is good; abstain from every form of evil. May the God of peace himself sanctify you entirely; and may your spirit and soul and body be kept sound and blameless at the coming of our Lord Jesus Christ. The one who calls you is faithful, and he will do this.*

1 THESSALONIANS 5:16–24

## PRAYER

I turn my heart to you, loving God, with my full attention and my complete desire. Forgive the times when I have forgotten to pray or prayed only for my own wants. Help me pray today not just with my lips but with my whole heart, and to hold fast to all that is good.

## ADVENT ACTION

"The Work of God" to which Benedict refers is the monastic practice of regular daily prayer. It is in our encounters with Scripture that God, and God's will for us, is revealed. Every day can be a birth to new life in God when our hearts are open to the sacred word. Take time to pray today at regular intervals. If you use a formal prayer, such as the psalms or rosary, try to keep your mind in harmony with your voice. Besides using traditional prayer words, make your prayer a conversation or a simple turning of your mind to some way in which Jesus is being manifested. If you don't think you have time for regular prayer, what about the minutes spent at traffic lights, in waiting lines, walking from place to place, doing routine chores? In each of these moments, simply ask that Jesus be born again in your heart.

## Christif With Many Faces

*L*et all guests who arrive be received as Christ, because He will say: "I was a stranger and you took Me in." And let due honor be shown to all, especially to those "of the household of the faith" and to wayfarers. When, therefore, a guest is announced, let him be met by the superior and the brethren with every mark of charity....In the greeting let all humility be shown to the guests, whether coming or going; with the head bowed down or the whole body prostrate on the ground, let Christ be adored in them as He is also received.

*RULE OF ST. BENEDICT*, 53:1–3, 6–7

## SCRIPTURE

*Let mutual love continue. Do not neglect to show hospitality to strangers, for by doing that some have entertained angels without knowing it.*

HEBREWS 13:1–2

## PRAYER

God, my most important guest, I want to welcome you with the honor you deserve. Help me to see you in everyone, especially those most difficult to welcome, so that my appreciation for them gives witness to your love, and my treatment of them helps them to see the wonder of your love.

## ADVENT ACTION

Every person we encounter is a little glimpse of the coming of Christ into the world. Some are easy to welcome, but others provide a great challenge. Yet each holds some revelation, some Word of God for us. At this season, there is much attention paid to the poor and homeless, and we rightly feel good when we help them. Strangers are one thing, but what about the familiar people? Sometimes it is much easier to give something to beggars, who will go away and leave both themselves and us with a positive glow, than it is to put up with that annoying person who appears over and over again at your desk or your backyard fence or your family dinner. If you know someone you find hard to welcome, say a special prayer for him or her today, and try to identify what you can learn about yourself or offer to God in those difficult encounters.

## DAY 10

# A Child Will Lead

*T*here was a man of venerable life who was blessed ("Benedictus") in both grace and name. From the time he was a boy, he had the heart of an elder. Leaving behind his literary studies, and relinquishing home and inheritance, he desired to please God alone and went to seek the monastic way of life. Thus he left Rome, learnedly ignorant and wisely unlearned.

*DIALOGUE II, PROLOGUE*

### SCRIPTURE

*And you, child, will be called the prophet of the Most High; for you will go before the Lord to prepare his ways, to give knowledge of salvation to his people by the forgiveness of*

*their sins. By the tender mercy of our God, the dawn from
on high will break upon us, to give light to those who sit in
darkness and in the shadow of death, to guide our feet into
the way of peace.*

LUKE 1:76–79

## PRAYER

God of Wisdom, you show your way to the innocent and
give wisdom to the least if we but follow your ways. Move
me from the intellectual to the spiritual center of myself.
Give me the open and childlike faith that will lead me to
greater love of you and to the joyous freedom to proclaim
your coming to the world.

## ADVENT ACTION

What did Jesus mean when he asked his followers to be
like children? Perhaps it is akin to what Gregory says
about Benedict. Knowledge can be the gateway to greater
spirituality, but sometimes our brains get in the way of
our hearts. We try to rationalize and organize mysteries
that are beyond us, or create explanations for things that
cannot be rationally parsed. We lose the ability for, or
are embarrassed by, the free expressions of joy and love
which children so unreservedly give. Can you think of a
time when you were taught or moved by the action of a
child or someone else considered "simple"?

# DAY 11

## Come to the Feast

*A*t that time, when there was a great famine in Campania, the man of God had given away all the possessions of the monastery to poor people, so that there was nothing left but a little oil in a glass jar. A certain subdeacon called Agapitus came to him, demanding that he be given a little oil. The servant of the Lord, who had resolved to give away everything on earth so that he might find all in heaven, commanded that the oil be given to him. The cellarer, however, did not do as he was ordered. When Benedict inquired whether the command had been carried out, the monk told him that he had not because there would not be any left for the monks. Then in anger, the abbot ordered the glass of oil to be thrown out the

window, so that nothing might remain in the monastery
contrary to obedience.

*DIALOGUES II*, XXVIII

SCRIPTURE

*On this mountain the LORD of hosts will make for all peoples
a feast of rich food, a feast of well-matured wines, of rich food
filled with marrow, of well-matured wines strained clear. And
he will destroy on this mountain the shroud that is cast over
all peoples, the sheet that is spread over all nations; he will
swallow up death for ever. Then the Lord GOD will wipe
away the tears from all faces, and the disgrace of his people he
will take away from all the earth, for the LORD has spoken.*

ISAIAH 25:6–8

PRAYER

All-generous God, you have nourished me in both body
and spirit. Thank you for your abundant gifts. Bless all
those who are hungry and all those who work to help
them. Help me to be bread for the world by using food
responsibly, sharing my bounty, and caring for the earth's
resources.

ADVENT ACTION

From Thanksgiving to New Year's Day, our celebrations
are marked by festive foods. We do not live by bread alone,
but it is nevertheless a necessary part of life and a symbol

of our relationships with others. As we enjoy these wonderful gifts, we must always remember their giver and our responsibility to those who do not have them. Take some food to a food pantry, make a contribution to a hunger charity, volunteer to deliver Christmas baskets or, when making your own special recipes, make some extra for a program that serves meals to the poor.

# Enough

*I*t is written, "Distribution was made to everyone according as he had need." We do not say by this that respect should be had for persons (God forbid), but regard for infirmities. Let those who have need of less thank God and not give way to sadness, but let the ones who have need of more humble themselves for their infirmity, and not be elated for the indulgence shown them; and thus all the members will be at peace. Above all, let not the evil of murmuring appear in the least word or sign for any reason whatever.

*RULE OF ST. BENEDICT*, 34:1–6

## SCRIPTURE

*They devoted themselves to the apostles' teaching and fellowship, to the breaking of bread and the prayers. Awe came upon everyone, because many wonders and signs were being done by the apostles. All who believed were together and had all things in common; they would sell their possessions and goods and distribute the proceeds to all, as any had need. Day by day, as they spent much time together in the temple, they broke bread at home and ate their food with glad and generous hearts, praising God and having the goodwill of all the people. And day by day the Lord added to their number those who were being saved.*

ACTS 2:42–47

## PRAYER

Provider God, in this season of gift lists, help me to remember that the greatest gifts are not bought with money. Give me a heart filled with gratitude for all you have done for me and a desire to let go of whatever possessions turn my attention from your love. Free me from envy of others and turn me instead to concern for those in need.

## ADVENT ACTION

Benedict turns the world's definition of success upside down. Our culture, especially in this season, tells us that we are valued by how much we can buy. We use our possessions to show ourselves and others how fortunate, special, beloved, and good we are. Benedict suggests that those who are free of possessions should be grateful that they don't need as much to prop themselves up. Those who have to be surrounded by more things or more special treatment are either genuinely infirm, and thus should receive extra care for their physical comfort, or are to be pitied for their emotional weakness, their lack of interior security. Take a look at your Christmas shopping list. Is there any place where you are overspending because of your own ego needs? Are you being tempted to get things you don't need because of advertising or peer pressure? Try to make your Christmas shopping a little more conscious this year, and don't forget sharing with the needy.

# Christic in the Captive

A Goth called Zalla...tortured a poor peasant to make him confess where his money was. Overcome by the torture, he said that he had given everything to Benedict, the servant of God....[B]inding his arms fast with strong cords, Zalla drove him in front of his horse to Benedict's...abbey, where they found him sitting at the entrance, reading a book....As he turned his eyes to the cords on the peasant, they miraculously fell from his arms more quickly than anyone could have undone them. When Zalla saw him suddenly freed, he fell to the ground, bowing down his stiff and cruel neck at the holy man's feet, and with humility commended himself to his prayers.

*DIALOGUES II, XXXI*

*The spirit of the Lord GOD is upon me, because the LORD has anointed me; he has sent me to bring good news to the oppressed, to bind up the broken-hearted, to proclaim liberty to the captives, and release to the prisoners; to proclaim the year of the LORD's favour, and the day of vengeance of our God; to comfort all who mourn; to provide for those who mourn in Zion—to give them a garland instead of ashes, the oil of gladness instead of mourning, the mantle of praise instead of a faint spirit. They will be called oaks of righteousness, the planting of the LORD, to display his glory. I will greatly rejoice in the LORD, my whole being shall exult in my God; for he has clothed me with the garments of salvation, he has covered me with the robe of righteousness, as a bridegroom decks himself with a garland, and as a bride adorns herself with her jewels. For as the earth brings forth its shoots, and as a garden causes what is sown in it to spring up so the Lord GOD will cause righteousness and praise to spring up before all the nations.*

ISAIAH 61:1–3, 10–11

PRAYER

God who lives in the suffering and oppressed, help me to see your presence in them. Let me bring your word to those who are in darkness and despair, and spread the good news of salvation. Bless especially today those held captive in any way. May your light shine upon them and free their hearts.

## ADVENT ACTION

Countless people are waiting for someone to release them from their chains. Each of these people is an image of the Christ who is waiting to be reborn in them. It might be an actual prisoner who is trying to repent and change, or political prisoners or hostages suffering for their beliefs, or a victim of human trafficking. Then there are those who are not bound by chains but by addiction, fear, or handicap. Do something today to loosen the bonds of another: Study or write regarding the penal system or some case of political oppression, learn more about modern forms of slavery, or contact a homebound or troubled person.

## Christic in the Sick

*Christ in the Sick*

*B*efore and above all things, care must be taken of
the sick, that they be served in very truth as Christ
is served; because He has said, "I was sick and you visited
Me" and "As long as you did it to one of these My least
brethren, you did it to Me." But let the sick themselves
also consider that they are served for the honor of God,
and let them not grieve their brethren who serve them by
unnecessary demands. These must, however, be patiently
borne with, because from such as these a more bountiful
reward is gained. Let the abbot's greatest concern, therefore, be that they suffer no neglect.

*RULE OF ST. BENEDICT, 36:1–6*

## SCRIPTURE

*Strengthen the weak hands, and make firm the feeble knees. Say to those who are of a fearful heart, 'Be strong, do not fear! Here is your God. He will come with vengeance, with terrible recompense. He will come and save you.' Then the eyes of the blind shall be opened, and the ears of the deaf unstopped; then the lame shall leap like a deer, and the tongue of the speechless sing for joy. For waters shall break forth in the wilderness, and streams in the desert.*

ISAIAH 35:3–6

## PRAYER

God of all who suffer, you wait for us to serve you in the sick and sorrowful. Bless all those who lack care or suffer with no one to love them. Help me to see your face in theirs and to share in your healing work by my love and generosity. Help me also to endure my own sufferings with patience and faith in your supporting presence.

## ADVENT ACTION

Jesus tells us that we should be alert, that he comes to us in many forms especially in those most needy. For both Jesus and Benedict, those who were infirm held a special place in their hearts. Sometimes it's hard to know what to do for a person who is sick, especially those in great pain or dying. There may be a feeling of awkwardness or helplessness but, once again, the poor and human face of

Christ is looking at us and we must look back. Benedict also acknowledges that not every sick person is a model of Christ-like suffering. In this season of anticipated joy, it is hard to be sick and unable to participate. The pain and disappointment can result in behavior that makes the illness harder on everyone. If you know someone who is sick or infirm from age, make a special effort to brighten their holidays. If you are fortunate enough not to know anyone who is sick, do something for a local hospital or nursing home.

## Love, Not Fear

*H*aving, therefore, ascended all these degrees of humility, the monk will presently arrive at that love of God, which being perfect, casts out fear. In virtue of this love all things which at first they observed not without fear, they will now begin to keep without any effort, and as it were, naturally by force of habit, no longer from the fear of hell, but from the love of Christ, from the very habit of good and the pleasure in virtue.

*RULE OF ST. BENEDICT, 7:67–70*

SCRIPTURE

*Sing aloud, O daughter Zion; shout, O Israel! Rejoice and exult with all your heart, O daughter Jerusalem! The LORD has taken away the judgements against you, he has turned away your enemies. The king of Israel, the LORD, is in your midst; you shall fear disaster no more. On that day it shall be said to Jerusalem: Do not fear, O Zion; do not let your hands grow weak. The LORD, your God, is in your midst, a warrior who gives victory; he will rejoice over you with gladness, he will renew you in his love; he will exult over you with loud singing as on a day of festival. I will remove disaster from you, so that you will not bear reproach for it.*

ZEPHANIAH 3:14–18

## PRAYER

God of joy, comfort those who cannot find joy in this season and help me to lighten their burdens in some small measure. Keep me mindful of what a happy thing it is to believe and trust in you. May others be drawn to you by seeing in my life the joy of my belief.

## ADVENT ACTION

The third Sunday of Advent is known as Gaudete Sunday, the day of rejoicing. It is the day on which the liturgy mitigates all the longing with a reminder that our hope is near at hand and we know that our Savior will indeed come. Benedict's deepest hope for his followers was that they not be unduly burdened. He truly believed that their sacrifices and discipline should not be about dread of a vengeful God, but the willing and eager response of someone who wants to please the one they love. Do something to bring joy to yourself and others today.

# *Wake Up*

*L*et us then rise at length, since the Scripture arouses us, saying: "It is now the hour for us to rise from sleep;" and having opened our eyes to the deifying light, let us hear with awestruck ears what the divine voice, crying out daily, admonishes us, saying: "Today, if you shall hear his voice, harden not your hearts."

*RULE OF ST. BENEDICT*, PROLOGUE: 8–10

## SCRIPTURE

*Besides this, you know what time it is, how it is now the moment for you to wake from sleep. For salvation is nearer to us now than when we became believers; the night is far gone,*

*the day is near. Let us then lay aside the works of darkness
and put on the armour of light.*

ROMANS 13:11–12

## PRAYER

God who is all Light, you have enlightened the world with
the coming of your son. Break into the darkness of my
indifference and weariness. Make me alert to the dawn of
new life that awaits me in each moment. Rouse my slug-
gish spirit to rejoice anew in you.

## ADVENT ACTION

We all have the best of intentions in our spiritual devel-
opment, especially in a season like Advent. Nevertheless,
there are so many things competing for our attention
and it's easy to lose our enthusiasm as real life interrupts.
We may not feel like we're making as much progress or
experiencing as much of a lift as we had hoped. Benedict
reminds his followers that every day is a new day, a chance
to begin again. Is there some area of your life where you
feel you've gotten lazy or just drowsy? Identify a particular
action you will take in the coming year to get yourself
moving forward again.

## DAY 17

## Run to the Light

And again: "He that has ears to hear let him hear what the Spirit says to the churches" [Revelation 2:7]. And what does He say?—"Come, children, listen to me, I will teach you the fear of the Lord" [Psalm 33(34):12]. "Run while you have the light of life, that the darkness of death overtake you not" [John 12:35].

*RULE OF ST. BENEDICT*, PROLOGUE: 11–13

### SCRIPTURE

*We are writing these things so that our joy may be complete. This is the message we have heard from him and proclaim to you, that God is light and in him there is no darkness at all. If we say that we have fellowship with him while we are walking in darkness, we lie and do not do what is true; but if we walk in the light as he himself is in the light, we have fellowship with one another, and the blood of Jesus his Son cleanses us from all sin.*

1 JOHN 1:4–7

## PRAYER

Goal of all my longing, I sometimes slow down or lose my way as I move towards you. Give me strength and endurance so that, even when death overtakes me, I will not be left in darkness, but will run into your loving arms and your eternal light.

## ADVENT ACTION

One of the distinctive things that Benedict does in his rule is to use words that have urgency. One does not merely saunter along the way, but is urged to run towards the light. Pay attention to light today. Each time you turn on a light or open a shade or move from a dim to a bright place, say a little prayer of thanksgiving for Jesus, the true light of the world.

## Guided by the Gospel

*W*hat, dearest brethren, can be sweeter to us than this voice of the Lord inviting us? See, in His loving kindness, the Lord shows us the way of life. Therefore, having our loins girt with faith and the performance of good works, let us walk His ways under the guidance of the Gospel, that we may be found worthy of seeing Him who hath called us to His kingdom.

*RULE OF ST. BENEDICT*, PROLOGUE: 19–21

SCRIPTURE

*As you know, we dealt with each one of you like a father with his children, urging and encouraging you and pleading that you should lead a life worthy of God, who calls you into his own kingdom and glory. We also constantly give thanks to God for this, that when you received the word of God that you heard from us, you accepted it not as a human word but as what it really is, God's word, which is also at work in you believers.*

1 THESSALONIANS 2:11–13

## PRAYER

God, you are constantly inviting me to listen to your voice. Help me to make time for conversation with you, to be attentive to the guidance of the Gospel, and to follow eagerly in your way. Make me always ready to turn your words into the action of good works until the day I am welcomed into the kingdom of heaven.

## ADVENT ACTION

In this passage, Benedict continues the image of moving forward in response to God's words. Athletes then, as now, girt themselves up in fitted clothing in order to move more quickly and freely. They also engage in serious daily training. Benedict thinks the most important exercise for the spiritually fit is to be guided by the Gospel. Read a chapter from the Gospel today, and try to make this a daily practice.

## Taking Time

*F*or every time we are led too far outside ourselves by the movement of our thoughts, we are not "with ourselves" even if we think we are, because we wander about and lose sight of ourselves.…We are carried out of ourselves in two ways, Peter. Either we fall under ourselves by sinful thoughts, or we are lifted above ourselves by the grace of contemplation.…Therefore, venerable Benedict in that solitary wilderness dwelt with himself, because he kept his thoughts within the cloister of his own soul. For when he was rapt in contemplation, he was lifted up, and unquestionably left himself behind.

*DIALOGUES II*, III

## SCRIPTURE

*O LORD, my heart is not lifted up, my eyes are not raised too high; I do not occupy myself with things too great and too marvellous for me. But I have calmed and quieted my soul, like a weaned child with its mother; my soul is like the weaned child that is with me. O Israel, hope in the LORD from this time on and for evermore.*

PSALM 131

## PRAYER

Enlightening God, lift me from my little thoughts about insignificant things and my grand thoughts about things beyond me. Whenever I feel tempted to think negatively about myself or others, help me to focus my attention on things that will raise me above myself. Be the center of my thoughts and the light of my mind forever.

## ADVENT ACTION

The word "contemplation" comes from a root that signifies time that is not "productive" in the worldly sense. It is simply taking time to be with what really matters. It is not unlike when we find our minds turning to some important event or experience with a loved one and simply bask in that recollection of goodness and happiness. Set aside some time today for your soul to waste in contemplation.

## Angels Watching

*I*f, therefore, the eyes of the Lord observe the good and the bad and the Lord always looks down from heaven on the children of earth, to see whether there be anyone that understands or seeks God; and if our actions are reported to the Lord day and night by the angels who are appointed to watch over us daily, we must ever be on our guard.

*RULE OF ST. BENEDICT, 7:26–29*

### SCRIPTURE

*"I will now declare the whole truth to you and will conceal nothing from you. Already I have declared it to you when I said, 'It is good to conceal the secret of a king, but to reveal*

*with due honour the works of God.' So now, when you and Sarah prayed, it was I who brought and read the record of your prayer before the glory of the Lord, and likewise whenever you buried the dead. And that time when you did not hesitate to get up and leave your dinner to go and bury the dead, I was sent to you to test you. And at the same time God sent me to heal you and Sarah your daughter-in-law. I am Raphael, one of the seven angels who stand ready and enter before the glory of the Lord." The two of them were shaken; they fell face down, for they were afraid. But he said to them, 'Do not be afraid; peace be with you. Bless God for evermore.*

TOBIT 12:11–17

## PRAYER

Ruler of the heavenly angels and all creation, you kindly pay attention to each person and protect us. Thank you for your "guardian angels," both the heavenly ones and the human ones who have helped me on my way. Help me to remember that your eyes are always upon me, especially when I lose sight of you.

## ADVENT ACTION

Angels show up a lot in the scriptures of Advent and Christmas. We tend to think of the angels as something like Santa's elves, making a list and checking it twice. Rather, Benedict is suggesting that all our acts are done in God's sight and, like a child wanting a parent's undivided attention, we should be eager to show what we can do and glad to have God watching. Pay attention throughout the day, and reflect at the end of the day on whether you did anything you'd rather God didn't hear about.

# *Silence*

*L*et us do what the Prophet says: "I said, I will take heed of my ways, that I sin not with my tongue: I have set a guard to my mouth, I was dumb, and was humbled, and kept silence even from good things." Here the prophet shows that, if at times we ought to refrain from useful speech for the sake of silence, how much more ought we to abstain from evil words on account of the punishment due to sin.

*RULE OF ST. BENEDICT, 6:1–2*

## SCRIPTURE

*He said, "Go out and stand on the mountain before the LORD, for the LORD is about to pass by." Now there was a great wind, so strong that it was splitting mountains and breaking rocks in pieces before the LORD, but the LORD was not in the wind; and after the wind an earthquake, but the LORD was not in the earthquake; and after the earthquake a fire, but the LORD was not in the fire; and after the fire a sound of sheer silence. When Elijah heard it, he wrapped his face in his mantle and went out and stood at the entrance of the cave. Then there came a voice to him that said, "What are you doing here, Elijah?"*

1 KINGS 19:11–13

## PRAYER

God of stillness, quiet my heart. Sometimes thunder and fire are less frightening than your presence. Empty me to hear you in those times when it is so easy to fill myself with the noise that distracts my attention, whether from outside or from my own thoughts and desires.

## ADVENT ACTION

Our lives are filled with sound, whether the noise of the world around us or the added sound from our electronic devices. Music is piped into waiting rooms, elevators, and anywhere else that quiet might otherwise sneak in. There always seems to be a TV on, a phone ringing, or earphones on our heads. Turn off some gadgets today. See if you can find a place where you can spend at least a few minutes in total silence. Afterwards, explore how it made you feel. What did you hear?

## *Here I Am*

*S*uch as these, therefore, instantly quitting their own work and giving up their own will, with hands disengaged, and leaving unfinished what they were doing, follow up, with the ready step of obedience, the word of command with deeds; and thus, as if in the same moment, both matters—the master's command and the disciple's finished work—are, in the swiftness of the fear of God, speedily finished together....Such as these truly live up to the maxim of the Lord in which He says: "I came not to do My own will, but the will of Him that sent Me."

*RULE OF ST. BENEDICT, 5:7–9, 13*

## SCRIPTURE

*In the sixth month the angel Gabriel was sent by God to a town in Galilee called Nazareth, to a virgin engaged to a man whose name was Joseph, of the house of David. The virgin's name was Mary. And he came to her and said, "Greetings, favoured one! The Lord is with you." But she was much perplexed by his words and pondered what sort of greeting this might be. The angel said to her, "Do not be afraid, Mary, for you have found favour with God. And now, you will conceive in your womb and bear a son, and you will name him Jesus. He will be great, and will be called the Son of the Most High, and the Lord God will give to him the throne of his ancestor David. He will reign over the house of Jacob for ever, and of his kingdom there will be no end." Mary said to the angel, "How can this be, since I am a virgin?" The angel said to her, "The Holy Spirit will come upon you, and the power of the Most High will overshadow you; therefore the child to be born will be holy; he will be called Son of God. And now, your relative Elizabeth in her old age has also conceived a son; and this is the sixth month for her who was said to be barren. For nothing will be impossible with God." Then Mary said, "Here am I, the servant of the Lord; let it be with me according to your word." Then the angel departed from her.*

LUKE 1:26–38

## PRAYER

Creator of all that exists, you call each of us to bring you into the world. Help me to cooperate with your will and to always choose what is good. Give me courage to accept what is asked of me when I am troubled and fearful. Give me hope when I think that what you ask is impossible. Help me to live my life according to your word and welcome your power within me.

## ADVENT ACTION

Through many kinds of messages and messengers, God often drops into our lives unexpectedly and, at times, inconveniently. Although Saint Benedict speaks of the perfect virtue of unhesitating obedience, we know that every human being, including Mary, feels some hesitation, especially when obedience will forever change our lives. Pay attention to the unexpected today. Recognize that God is in every moment, and try to welcome the interruptions, the inconveniences, the adjustments. Pick one to reflect on at the end of the day. How did you respond to it and what did you receive from it?

# Humility

*T*he Holy Scripture cries to us saying: "Every one that exalts himself shall be humbled; and he that humbles himself shall be exalted." Since, therefore, it says this, it shows us that every exaltation is a kind of pride. The Prophet declares that he guards himself against this, saying: "Lord, my heart is not puffed up; nor are my eyes haughty. Neither have I walked in great matters nor in wonderful things above me."

*RULE OF ST. BENEDICT, 7:1–3*

## SCRIPTURE

*Then Mary said, "Here am I, the servant of the Lord; let it be with me according to your word." Then the angel departed from her. And Mary said, "My soul magnifies the Lord, and my spirit rejoices in God my Saviour, for he has looked with favour on the lowliness of his servant. Surely, from now on all generations will call me blessed; for the Mighty One has done great things for me, and holy is his name. His mercy is for those who fear him from generation to generation. He has shown strength with his arm; he has scattered the proud in the thoughts of their hearts. He has brought down the powerful from their thrones, and lifted up the lowly."*

LUKE 1:38, 46–52

## PRAYER

God of power and might, you stoop down to tenderly embrace the humble. It is only in knowing how small I am that I can sense how great you are. Help me to remember the source of all good gifts and to proclaim my gratitude and dependence in all that I do.

## ADVENT ACTION

Many have the mistaken notion that humility has to do with low self-esteem or never thinking positively about one's self. Rather, humility is a right perspective. It acknowledges that God is God, and I am not. If we did not have gifts from God, we could never magnify the Lord so that others could see the wonders God does and, by seeing this human life, be able to call God blessed. Take time today to think about how you respond to compliments. Thank God for your gifts and commit yourself to their holy and humble use.

# Christ Visits

*H*is sister called Scholastica, dedicated from her infancy to our Lord, used to come once a year to visit her brother. The man of God would come down to visit her in a house owned by the monastery not far from the gate. One year she came as usual and her venerable brother went to meet her with his disciples. They spent the whole day in the praises of God and spiritual conversation, and when the darkness of night had almost fallen, they took a meal together. As they were still sitting at the table, talking about holy things, and the hour became late, the holy nun his sister asked him to stay saying, "Please do not leave tonight, but let us speak until morning of the joys of heaven."

*DIALOGUES II, XXXIII*

## SCRIPTURE

*In those days Mary set out and went with haste to a Judean town in the hill country, where she entered the house of Zechariah and greeted Elizabeth. When Elizabeth heard Mary's greeting, the child leapt in her womb. And Elizabeth was filled with the Holy Spirit and exclaimed with a loud cry, "Blessed are you among women, and blessed is the fruit of your womb. And why has this happened to me, that the mother of my Lord comes to me? For as soon as I heard the sound of your greeting, the child in my womb leapt for joy. And blessed is she who believed that there would be a fulfilment of what was spoken to her by the Lord."*

LUKE 1:39–45

## PRAYER

Creator God, you did not make us to be alone. Thank you for the blessings of friends and family. Help me to reach out to others, to make the effort to be with them, whether in body, spirit, or prayer. Make of my presence a coming of the Lord, so that their hearts will leap with the joy of having seen you through my caring presence.

## ADVENT ACTION

We rejoice when we see the face of someone we love. Christmas is often a special time of visits and reunions. There are cards and greetings from people far away. This spirit of connection is not simply between human beings, but is a reflection of our unity in the one family of God's creation. Take some time in this season to re-connect with someone you have neglected or from whom you have been distanced.

# DAY 25

## Trusting

*H*oly ones, as much as they are one with God, are not ignorant of the mind of God. For all who devoutly follow God, are also one with God by their devotion; but those who are weighed down by the flesh are not wholly with God. As they are joined with God, they know the hidden things of God, but as far as they are separated from God, they do not know them. Because they cannot yet perfectly penetrate the secrets, they call God's judgments incomprehensible. But those who are joined to him in spirit, since they accept what they find in the holy scripture and private revelations, recognize, own and utter these things. What God does not teach, they do not know; what God teaches, they know.

*DIALOGUES II*, 16:7

## SCRIPTURE

*Now the birth of Jesus the Messiah took place in this way. When his mother Mary had been engaged to Joseph, but before they lived together, she was found to be with child from the Holy Spirit. Her husband Joseph, being a righteous man and unwilling to expose her to public disgrace, planned to dismiss her quietly. But just when he had resolved to do this, an angel of the Lord appeared to him in a dream and said, "Joseph, son of David, do not be afraid to take Mary as your wife, for the child conceived in her is from the Holy Spirit. She will bear a son, and you are to name him Jesus, for he will save his people from their sins."*

MATTHEW 1:18–21

## PRAYER

God of Wisdom, you enlighten the hearts and minds of those who believe your words. Give me the insight to know what you want of me, especially when it defies the world's way of seeing. Help me to cooperate in bringing Jesus to a world which may not understand my choices. As Joseph supported Mary and Jesus, may my faith in your promises be a source of support to others and a witness of love for your son.

## ADVENT ACTION

Saint Gregory explains that no one can totally know God's will because we are only human. He does, however, point out that we can, through our own openness and prayer, be more attuned to seeing the world as God sees it. Joseph had to make a difficult choice, letting his faith and God's promise override common sense and public ridicule. Is there something you need to do to challenge an injustice or make a hard choice? Is "what others might think" keeping you from following a call from God? Try to take some small step toward following the inner voice that leads to holiness.

# DAY 26

## Jacob's Ladder

*H*ence, brethren, if we wish to reach the greatest height of humility, and speedily to arrive at that heavenly exaltation to which ascent is made in the present life by humility, then, mounting by our actions, we must erect the ladder which appeared to Jacob in his dream, by means of which angels were shown to him ascending and descending. Without a doubt, we understand this ascending and descending to be nothing else but that we descend by pride and ascend by humility.

*RULE OF ST. BENEDICT, 7:5-7*

*Let the same mind be in you that was in Christ Jesus, who, though he was in the form of God, did not regard equality with God as something to be exploited, but emptied himself, taking the form of a slave, being born in human likeness. And being found in human form, he humbled himself and became obedient to the point of death—even death on a cross. Therefore God also highly exalted him and gave him the name that is above every name, so that at the name of Jesus every knee should bend, in heaven and on earth and under the earth, and every tongue should confess that Jesus Christ is Lord, to the glory of God the Father.*

PHILIPPIANS 2:5–11

## PRAYER

You who are all powerful chose to share in our humanity through your Son Jesus. May I remember that I must also be at the humble service of others. Keep me mindful that the place where heaven and earth meet is wherever I allow heavenly power to come down through me.

## ADVENT ACTION

Jesus told his disciples that they must be the servants of all, and he was a model of humility in his service to others. The opposite attitude is one of exaltation. As Advent ends, have there been times in this season when this attitude crept in? Ask forgiveness today for any occasions in which you took too much pride or were too concerned about: being invited to the right parties, looking better than others, giving or receiving the best gifts, acquiring other status symbols.

## Body and Soul

*T*he erected ladder, however, is our life in the present world, which, if the heart is humble, is by the Lord lifted up to heaven. For we say that our body and our soul are the two sides of this ladder; and into these sides the divine calling hath inserted various degrees of humility or discipline which we must mount.

*RULE OF ST. BENEDICT, 7:8–9*

SCRIPTURE

*The true light, which enlightens everyone, was coming into the world. He was in the world, and the world came into being through him; yet the world did not know him. He came to what was his own, and his own people did not accept him.*

*But to all who received him, who believed in his name, he gave power to become children of God, who were born, not of blood or of the will of the flesh or of the will of man, but of God. And the Word became flesh and lived among us, and we have seen his glory, the glory as of a father's only son, full of grace and truth.*

JOHN 1:9–14

## PRAYER

Creator, you made me in your image and you saw that it was good. You even gave your Son our fragile human flesh. Help me to use my own body and soul to share in his saving work. As he walked among us and experienced birth and suffering and death, may I obediently fulfill your will in my own earthly being.

## ADVENT ACTION

Being made of body and soul is a marvelous thing. Our fleshly body is our way of relating to other human beings, of learning, worshipping, serving, and of all the other actions that give glory to God. As you think about Jesus being Word made flesh, thank God for your own mortal flesh. Reflect especially on how you treat it, whether you are attentive to its needs, whether you accept it in a humble and realistic way, and how you use or misuse it.

## Of Lowly Birth

*T*he sixth degree of humility is, when a monk is
content with the meanest and worst of everything.

RULE OF ST. BENEDICT, 7:49

### SCRIPTURE

*For God's foolishness is wiser than human wisdom, and
God's weakness is stronger than human strength. Consider
your own call, brothers and sisters: not many of you were wise
by human standards, not many were powerful, not many
were of noble birth. But God chose what is foolish in the world
to shame the wise; God chose what is weak in the world to
shame the strong; God chose what is low and despised in
the world, things that are not, to reduce to nothing things*

*that are, so that no one might boast in the presence of God.*
*He is the source of your life in Christ Jesus, who became for*
*us wisdom from God, and righteousness and sanctification*
*and redemption, in order that, as it is written, "Let the one*
*who boasts, boast in the Lord."*

1 CORINTHIANS 1:25–31

## PRAYER

God of the lowly, I find it hard when I am not comfortable
or when I feel I have been treated unfairly. Help me to
remember the conditions under which your own beloved
son Jesus was born, and to offer my own suffering for
those who suffer more and have no one to pray for them.

## ADVENT ACTION

Jesus could have come in any way, but he came in the
lowliest of circumstances, of a rejected people in total pov-
erty and dependence. Human neediness would continue
throughout his life even to a brutal and unjust execution.
Think of a time when you felt helpless in the face of unfair
circumstances. Try to accept this, think of some good
that might have come from it, and pray for healing of any
resentment that might remain, as you welcome Jesus to
be born anew in your heart.

# PART II
~~~~~~

# READINGS
# FOR THE
# CHRISTMAS
# SEASON

# Light of the World

*While the brothers were still asleep, the man of God, Benedict, was keeping vigil before the time of the night Office. Standing at the window of his cell, and praying to almighty God, he suddenly saw in the dead of the night, as he looked forth, a light so bright that all the darkness of the night was dispelled. The light that shone in the midst of darkness was far brighter than the light of the day.*

DIALOGUES II, XXXV

## SCRIPTURE

*For a child has been born for us, a son given to us; authority rests upon his shoulders; and he is named*

*Wonderful Counsellor, Mighty God, Everlasting Father,*
*Prince of Peace. His authority shall grow continually,*
*and there shall be endless peace for the throne of David*
*and his kingdom. He will establish and uphold it with*
*justice and with righteousness from this time onwards*
*and for evermore. The zeal of the LORD of hosts will do*
*this.*

ISAIAH 9:6–7

## PRAYER

I rejoice this day, O God, for having received the wondrous gift of your Word made flesh. Thank you for loving the world and all its creatures so much. May I always be alert to his presence among us, and may he be born anew in my heart so that I might show his presence to others and find joy every day in my salvation.

## ADVENT ACTION

Jesus, the Light of the World, dwells among us. Make this day a day of holiness in your celebration. If possible, go to church to celebrate with other believers. Spend some time in private prayer as well, perhaps with the nativity narrative in the Bible or before a manger scene or image of the Madonna and infant. Try also to help those around you remember the true reason for the celebration and the good news of salvation.

## DAY 2

# The Witness of Stephen

*T*he next day the venerable woman returned to her monastery, and the man of God to his monastery. Three days later, standing in his cell, and lifting his eyes to heaven, he saw the soul of his sister depart from her body and ascend into heaven in the likeness of a dove. Rejoicing much to see her great glory, he gave thanks to almighty God with hymns and praise, and announced the news of her death to the brothers.

*DIALOGUES II, XXXIV*

## SCRIPTURE

*[Stephen said] "They killed those who foretold the coming of the Righteous One, and now you have become his betrayers*

*and murderers. You are the ones that received the law as ordained by angels, and yet you have not kept it." When they heard these things, they became enraged and ground their teeth at Stephen. But filled with the Holy Spirit, he gazed into heaven and saw the glory of God and Jesus standing at the right hand of God. "Look," he said, "I see the heavens opened and the Son of Man standing at the right hand of God!"*

ACTS 7:52–56

## PRAYER

Loving God, in all the ages since the birth of your son, men and women have lived their lives proclaiming him and have died knowing their salvation is assured in him. Help me to walk in the way of the saints, giving witness to you through all the days of my life and facing fearlessly the death that will bring me to eternal life in you.

## ADVENT ACTION

Immediately after Christmas, the Church celebrates the death of Stephen. The message is that all people are called through Jesus to witness to his life and its transformation of the world. Think about a person in your own life whom you believed to be saintly. Think about what it was that made him or her so special and how you can imitate those virtues in your own life.

# DAY 3

## John's Good News

*T*he one that hastens on to the perfection of the religious life, has at hand the teachings of the holy Fathers, the observance of which leads one to the height of perfection. For what page or what utterance of the divinely inspired books of the Old and the New Testament is not a most exact rule of human life?

*RULE OF ST. BENEDICT, 73:2–3*

SCRIPTURE

*This is the disciple who is testifying to these things and has written them, and we know that his testimony is true. But there are also many other things that Jesus did; if every one of them were written down, I suppose that the world itself could not contain the books that would be written.*

JOHN 21:24–25

## PRAYER

Eternal Word, you have given us the Gospels to show us how you would have us live. Help me to love you as the first disciples did and, without seeing you in the flesh, to know that it is you to whom we must go and whom we must follow.

## ADVENT ACTION

Saint John the Evangelist, whose feast is commemorated on the second day after Christmas, is honored for his role in telling the story of Jesus in both his humanity and divinity. Read and meditate upon some portion of the Gospel of John today.

## DAY 4

# Holy Innocents

*A*lthough human nature is of itself drawn to feel compassion for these life periods, namely, old age and childhood, still, let the decree of the Rule make provision also for them. Let their natural weakness be always taken into account and let the strictness of the Rule not be kept with them.

*RULE OF ST. BENEDICT, 37:1–2*

## SCRIPTURE

*When Herod saw that he had been tricked by the wise men, he was infuriated, and he sent and killed all the children in and around Bethlehem who were two years old or under, according to the time that he had learned from the wise men. Then was fulfilled what had been spoken through the prophet Jeremiah: "A voice was heard in Ramah, wailing and loud lamentation, Rachel weeping for her children; she refused to be consoled, because they are no more."*

MATTHEW 2:16–18

## PRAYER

God of the innocent, so many people suffer in our world who are powerless to defend themselves. Help me to be attentive to those who are most vulnerable and to never allow my own power to be used in a harmful way. Bless the children, the frail, and all victims of the rage of others.

## ADVENT ACTION

The third day after Christmas traditionally commemorates the Holy Innocents. They were not martyred for Jesus because of their own proclamation of faith, like Stephen, but were the first to die because of Jesus' entry into the world. Write a letter to a legislator, study about an issue, or contribute to a cause that advocates for the needs of innocent children: Education, abortion, welfare, child labor, etc.

## Shining Star

*A* marvelous thing followed for, as he himself later reported, the whole world was gathered together before his eyes as if in a single ray of the sun....[Gregory says] To the soul that beholds the Creator, all other creatures seem narrow by comparison. No matter how little of the Creator's light with which one sees, all other created things seem very small. By that interior light of contemplation, the capacity of the soul becomes greater, and it is so expanded in God that it is above the world. Rapt in the light of God, it is raised up and enlarged. When it is so exalted and looks downward, it comprehends how little all creation is.

*DIALOGUES II, XXXV*

## SCRIPTURE

*When they had heard the king, they set out; and there, ahead of them, went the star that they had seen at its rising, until it stopped over the place where the child was. When they saw that the star had stopped, they were overwhelmed with joy.*

MATTHEW 2:9–10

## PRAYER

God of Light, just as the star shone over the infant Jesus and drew the wise to him, you shed your light on all your creatures and invite me to see that we are one in you. Enlighten my heart and mind; raise me above myself so that I may see everything and everyone in your light.

## ADVENT ACTION

No place in the *Dialogue* of Gregory does the biographical narrative mesh so well with the Benedict behind the *Rule* than in the story of his vision of light. Here was a man who truly understood the meaning of life. Each moment is part of a divine totality. As the light was in the sky at Jesus' birth, the light of God illuminates everything that exists. Pick some small moments today, perhaps the same time each hour, and visualize whatever you are doing, or the object or person in front of you, as bathed in a divine light.

## DAY 6

# Peace on Earth

*A*s there is a harsh and evil zeal which separates from God and leads to hell, so there is a virtuous zeal which separates from vice and leads to God and life everlasting. Let the monks, therefore, practice this zeal with most ardent love; namely, that in honor they outrun one another. Let them bear their infirmities, whether of body or mind, with the utmost patience; let them vie with one another in obedience. Let no one follow what he thinks useful to himself, but rather to another. Let them practice fraternal charity with a chaste love.

*RULE OF ST. BENEDICT, 72:1–9*

## SCRIPTURE

*Righteousness shall be the belt around his waist, and faithfulness the belt around his loins. The wolf shall live with the lamb, the leopard shall lie down with the kid, the calf and the lion and the fatling together, and a little child shall lead them. The cow and the bear shall graze, their young shall lie down together; and the lion shall eat straw like the ox. The nursing child shall play over the hole of the asp, and the weaned child shall put its hand on the adder's den. They will not hurt or destroy on all my holy mountain; for the earth will be full of the knowledge of the Lord as the waters cover the sea.*

ISAIAH 11:5–9

## PRAYER

Forgiving and reconciling God, we have hurt you in many ways with our human tendency to violence and discord. Bless those who are living face to face with hatred and war today. As your son came to be the Prince of Peace, make me a peacemaker in my heart, my home, and my world.

## ADVENT ACTION

There has probably never been a day in this world, even after Christ brought his message of peace, in which all people lived without violence. Ask yourself why it seems so easy to strike out at others. Who are your enemies? Who do you believe is unable to walk together like the lion and the lamb in the new kingdom? What can you do to change this?

# Babe in Arms

$\mathcal{W}$hen he has placed [the profession document] there, let the novice next begin the verse: "Receive me, O Lord, according to your word and I shall live; and let me not be disappointed in my expectations." Then let all the brothers repeat this verse three times, adding the *Gloria Patri*. Then let that novice brother cast himself down at the feet of all, that they may pray for him; and from that day let him be counted in the brotherhood.

*RULE OF ST. BENEDICT, 58:21–23*

## SCRIPTURE

*Now there was a man in Jerusalem whose name was Simeon; this man was righteous and devout, looking forward to the consolation of Israel, and the Holy Spirit rested on him. It had been revealed to him by the Holy Spirit that he would not see death before he had seen the Lord's Messiah. Guided by the Spirit, Simeon came into the temple; and when the parents brought in the child Jesus, to do for him what was customary under the law, Simeon took him in his arms and praised God, saying, "Master, now you are dismissing your servant in peace, according to your word; for my eyes have seen your salvation, which you have prepared in the presence of all peoples, a light for revelation to the Gentiles and for glory to your people Israel."*

LUKE 2:25–32

## PRAYER

God of the Promise, you continue to be my hope. The world has known the earthly coming of your Son, and I look forward to seeing him at the end of my own earthly life. Bless all those who do not feel sustained and fulfilled in their lives and help me to be comforted in all my doubts by the belief that you live and reign forever.

## ADVENT ACTION

Simeon was lucky to actually hold and recognize the infant Jesus. The rest of us have to be satisfied believing that we will someday see Him. When the monastic makes profession and sings the prayer Benedict prescribes above, he or she does so with raised arms. It is a gesture like that of a small child wanting to be picked up, carried, embraced. We must believe, like Simeon, that we have seen the light of salvation and can carry on without doubting the source of our hopes. Try praying for a short time with raised arms or hands outstretched in front of you. How does it feel to throw yourself open to God and to hope that God will respond? Try to feel God's embrace as you pray.

## New Beginnings

*T*he Lord fulfilling these words waits for us from day
to day, that we respond to His holy admonitions by
our works.

*RULE OF ST. BENFDICT,* PROLOGUE: 35

### SCRIPTURE

*The LORD spoke to Moses, saying: Speak to Aaron and his
sons, saying, Thus you shall bless the Israelites: You shall say
to them, The LORD bless you and keep you; the LORD make
his face to shine upon you, and be gracious to you; the LORD
lift up his countenance upon you, and give you peace. So they
shall put my name on the Israelites, and I will bless them.*

NUMBERS 6:22–27

## PRAYER

Thank you God for this new year and all that it might hold. Open my heart to embrace its mysteries, especially the days which will be difficult, and to remember that each day is a gift from you. I offer this day, this year, and my whole life to you.

## ADVENT ACTION

Benedict reminds his followers that each day is a new beginning, a chance to renew the covenant we have made with God. Benedict believes the question "Who longs for life?" is asked every day, and every day offers a new opportunity to respond positively. New Year's resolutions may be a cliché, but the new year is an opportunity to think about new beginnings. Make a very short and realistic list this year, keep it where you will see it often, and check your progress (or lack!) regularly. Benedict reminds us not to dwell on it, but to thank God if today was good, ask forgiveness if it wasn't, and start all over again tomorrow.

## DAY 9

# Everything Is Sacred

*L*et him regard all the vessels of the monastery and all its substance, as if they were sacred vessels of the altar. Let him neglect nothing and let him not give way to avarice, nor let him be wasteful and a squanderer of the goods of the monastery.

*RULE OF ST. BENEDICT, 31:10–12*

## SCRIPTURE

*On that day there shall be inscribed on the bells of the horses, "Holy to the LORD." And the cooking-pots in the house of the LORD shall be as holy as the bowls in front of the altar; and every cooking-pot in Jerusalem and Judah shall be sacred to the LORD of hosts, so that all who sacrifice may come and use*

*...em to boil the flesh of the sacrifice. And there shall no lon-*
*ger be traders in the house of the LORD of hosts on that day.*

ZECHARIAH 14:20–21

## PRAYER

God of all things, the birth of your son has shown us the way to life in the new Jerusalem. In your kingdom, every-thing is sacred and holds your presence. Help me to do my part to restore the right order of the world by making every act and object sacred to you.

## ADVENT ACTION

Benedict did not believe that there was any unimport-ant act or object. All was part of the sacred creation and required reverence. Do something for the earth today or do some ordinary task in a more mindful way.

# DAY 10

## *Listen*

*L*isten, O my son, to the precepts of your master, and incline the ear of your heart, and cheerfully receive and faithfully execute the admonitions of your loving Father, that by the toil of obedience you may return to Him from whom by the sloth of disobedience you have gone away. To you, therefore, my speech is now directed, who, giving up your own will, take up the strong and most excellent arms of obedience, to do battle for Christ the Lord, the true King.

*RULE OF ST. BENEDICT, 1--3*

### SCRIPTURE

*[Then Zechariah said] "Blessed be the Lord God of Israel, for he has looked favourably on his people and redeemed*

*them. He has raised up a mighty saviour for us in the house of his servant David, as he spoke through the mouth of his holy prophets from of old, that we would be saved from our enemies and from the hand of all who hate us. Thus he has shown the mercy promised to our ancestors, and has remembered his holy covenant, the oath that he swore to our ancestor Abraham, to grant us that we, being rescued from the hands of our enemies, might serve him without fear, in holiness and righteousness before him all our days."*

LUKE 1:68–75

## PRAYER

Almighty One, I praise you for having raised up a savior for us in our weak world. Give me renewed strength and faith to proclaim your wonderful salvation and to listen with my whole heart to your loving instructions.

## ADVENT ACTION

The first word of the Rule is "listen." The Savior has come to us and all of life is transformed by that wonder. Much of the time, however, we do not think about it. If we really listen, we can hear the Good News all around us in people and events and the beauty of the world. Practice attentive listening today: A deep conversation, a piece of music, the sounds of nature. Try to hear God speaking.

# DAY 11

## *Holiness*

*D*o not desire to be called holy before one is, but to be holy first, that one may be truly so called. Fulfill daily the commandments of God by works...hate no one...and never despair of God's mercy.

RULE OF ST. BENEDICT, 4: 62–63, 74

### SCRIPTURE

*Blessed be the God and Father of our Lord Jesus Christ, who has blessed us in Christ with every spiritual blessing in the heavenly places, just as he chose us in Christ before the foundation of the world to be holy and blameless before him in love. He destined us for adoption as his children through Jesus Christ, according to the good pleasure of his will, to the praise of his glorious grace that he freely bestowed on us in the Beloved. In him we have redemption through his blood, the forgiveness of our trespasses, according to the riches of his grace that he lavished on us. With all wisdom and insight he has made known to us the mystery of his will, according to his good pleasure that he set forth in Christ, as a plan for the fullness of time, to gather up all things in him, things in heaven and things on earth. In Christ we have also obtained an inheritance, having been destined according to the purpose of him who accomplishes all things according to his counsel and will, so that we, who were the first to set our hope on Christ, might live for the praise of his glory.*

EPHESIANS 1:3–12

PRAYER

God who graciously gave us Jesus and calls us to be your children, I praise you for the grace you have lavished upon me. Bless all those who do not know your love in their lives and those who are burdened by loneliness and despair. I pray that I may grow in holiness each day and know that you are with me. Keep me mindful of your presence at all times, help me see your son Jesus in everyone, that I might help to bring his kingdom to the world.

## ADVENT ACTION

As the Christmas season ends, the glow of peace and goodwill quickly fades. What does it mean to be holy in day-to-day life? Make a list of what you think a holy person is and does. What practices would help you be like that? How can you see the world in a more holy way?

## Epiphany

*L*et them prefer nothing whatever to Christ, and may
He lead us all together to life everlasting.

*RULE OF ST. BENEDICT, 72:11–12*

### SCRIPTURE

*Arise, shine; for your light has come, and the glory of the
LORD has risen upon you. For darkness shall cover the earth,
and thick darkness the peoples; but the LORD will arise upon
you, and his glory will appear over you. Nations shall come
to your light, and kings to the brightness of your dawn. Lift
up your eyes and look around; they all gather together, they
come to you; your sons shall come from far away, and your
daughters shall be carried on their nurses' arms. Then you*

*shall see and be radiant; your heart shall thrill and rejoice, because the abundance of the sea shall be brought to you, the wealth of the nations shall come to you.*

ISAIAH 60:1–5

## PRAYER

God of all nations, the light of your son's birth gathered the rich and the lowly, the nearby and the foreigner. Bless all the nations and peoples of the world with your love and peace. May I stand in awe before this mystery in this season and every day of my life until we are all gathered together into your kingdom.

## ADVENT ACTION

The next major feast of the Church after New Year's Day is Epiphany. This feast recognizes that Jesus was to be not just a Jew among Jews, but the Savior of all peoples. In the coming weeks, try to get to know someone who is not of your faith, or a person who is foreign-born, or of a very different culture or lifestyle. Make an attempt to really learn about the other, not to convert or criticize, but to stand together in the light which shines on the whole human family. Celebrate what you have in common with each person you meet rather than focusing on how you are different. Having joyfully welcomed the Christ Child this Christmas, remember to welcome each person as Christ.

# PART III

# FORMATS

## for

# NIGHTLY PRAYER

## and

# READING

# Formats for
# Nightly Prayer and Reading

THE PURPOSE OF PRESENTING two optional formats for nightly readings and prayer is to offer ways to use the material in this book for group or individual prayer. Of course, there are other ways in which to use this book—for example, as a meditative daily reader or as a guide for a prayer journal—but the following familiar liturgical formats provide a structure that can be used in a variety of contexts.

## ⁜⁜⁜ FORMAT 1 ⁜⁜⁜⁜⁜⁜⁜⁜⁜⁜⁜⁜⁜⁜⁜⁜⁜⁜⁜⁜

### OPENING PRAYER

The observance begins with these words:

*God, come to my assistance.*
*Lord, make haste to help me.*

followed by:

*Glory to the Father, and to the Son,*
*and to the Holy Spirit, as it was in the beginning,*
*is now, and will be for ever. Amen. Alleluia.*

### EXAMINATION OF CONSCIENCE

If this observance is being prayed individually, an examination of conscience may be included. Here is a short examination of conscience; you may, of course, use your own preferred method.

1. Place yourself in a quiet frame of mind.
2. Review your life since your last confession.
3. Reflect on the Ten Commandments and any sins against these commandments.
4. Reflect on the words of the gospel, especially Jesus' commandment to love your neighbor as yourself.
5. Ask yourself these questions: How have I been unkind in thoughts, words, and actions? Am I refusing to forgive anyone? Do I despise any group or person? Am I a prisoner of fear, anxiety, worry, guilt, inferiority, or hatred of myself?

## PENITENTIAL RITE (OPTIONAL)

If a group of people are praying in unison, a penitential rite from the *Roman Missal* may be used:

*Presider:* Lord Jesus, you came to call all people to yourself: Lord, have mercy.

*All:* Lord, have mercy.

*Presider:* Lord Jesus, you come to us in word and prayer: Christ, have mercy.

*All:* Christ, have mercy.

*Presider:* Lord Jesus, you will appear in glory with all your saints:
Lord, have mercy.

*All:* Lord, have mercy.

*Presider:* May almighty God have mercy on us, forgive us our sins, and bring us to life everlasting.

*All:* Amen.

## HYMN: "O COME, O COME, EMMANUEL"

A hymn is now sung or recited. This Advent hymn is a paraphrase of the great "O" Antiphons written in the twelfth century and translated by John Mason Neale in 1852.

> O come, O come, Emmanuel,
> And ransom captive Israel;
> That mourns in lonely exile here,
> Until the Son of God appear.

> *Refrain:*  Rejoice! Rejoice! O Israel
>             To thee shall come, Emmanuel!

> O come, thou wisdom, from on high,
> And order all things far and nigh;
> To us the path of knowledge show,
> And teach us in her ways to go.

> *Refrain*

> O come, O come, thou Lord of might,
> Who to thy tribes on Sinai's height
> In ancient times did give the law,
> In cloud, and majesty, and awe.

> *Refrain*

> O come, thou rod of Jesse's stem,
> From ev'ry foe deliver them
> That trust thy mighty power to save,
> And give them vict'ry o'er the grave.

*Refrain*

O come, thou key of David, come,
And open wide our heav'nly home,
Make safe the way that leads on high,
That we no more have cause to sigh.

*Refrain*

O come, thou Dayspring from on high,
And cheer us by thy drawing nigh;
Disperse the gloomy clouds of night
And death's dark shadow put to flight.

*Refrain*

O come, Desire of nations, bind
In one the hearts of all mankind;
Bid every strife and quarrel cease
And fill the world with heaven's peace.

*Refrain*

## PSALM 27:7–14—GOD STANDS BY US IN DANGERS

Hear, O LORD, when I cry aloud,
  be gracious to me and answer me!
"Come," my heart says, "seek his face!"
  Your face, LORD, do I seek.
  Do not hide your face from me.

Do not turn your servant away in anger,
  you who have been my help.
Do not cast me off, do not forsake me,
  O God of my salvation!
If my father and mother forsake me,
  the LORD will take me up.

Teach me your way, O LORD,
  and lead me on a level path
  because of my enemies.
Do not give me up to the will of my adversaries,
  for false witnesses have risen against me,
  and they are breathing out violence.

I believe that I shall see the goodness of the LORD
  in the land of the living.
Wait for the LORD;
  be strong, and let your heart take courage;
  wait for the LORD!

## RESPONSE

I long to see your face, O Lord. You are my light and my help. Do not turn away from me.

## SCRIPTURE READING

Read silently or have a presider proclaim the Scripture of the day that is selected.

## RESPONSE

Come and set us free, Lord God of power and might. Let your face shine on us and we will be saved.

*Glory to the Father, and to the Son,*
*and to the Holy Spirit:*
*as it was in the beginning, is now,*
*and will be for ever. Amen.*

## SECOND READING

Read the excerpt from Saint Benedict for the day selected.

## CANTICLE OF SIMEON

Lord, now you let your servant go in peace;
your word has been fulfilled:
my own eyes have seen the salvation
which you have prepared in the sight of every people:
a light to reveal you to the nations
and the glory of your people Israel.

Glory to the Father, and to the Son, and to the Holy Spirit:
as it was in the beginning, is now,
and will be for ever. Amen.

## PRAYER

Say the prayer that follows the day's selected excerpt from
Saint Benedict.

## BLESSING

May the all-powerful Lord grant us a restful night and a peaceful
death. Amen.

## MARIAN ANTIPHON

Loving mother of the Redeemer,
gate of heaven, star of the sea,
assist your people who have fallen yet strive to rise again.
To the wonderment of nature you bore your Creator,
yet remained a virgin after as before.
You who received Gabriel's joyful greeting,
have pity on us poor sinners.

## FORMAT 2

### OPENING PRAYER

The observance begins with these words:

*God, come to my assistance.*
*Lord, make haste to help me.*

followed by:

*Glory to the Father, and to the Son,*
*and to the Holy Spirit, as it was in the beginning,*
*is now, and will be for ever. Amen. Alleluia.*

### EXAMINATION OF CONSCIENCE

If this observance is being prayed individually, an examination of conscience may be included. Here is a short examination of conscience; you may, of course, use your own preferred method.

1. Place yourself in a quiet frame of mind.
2. Review your life since your last confession.
3. Reflect on the Ten Commandments and any sins against these commandments.
4. Reflect on the words of the gospel, especially Jesus' commandment to love your neighbor as yourself.
5. Ask yourself these questions: How have I been unkind in thoughts, words, and actions? Am I refusing to forgive anyone? Do I despise any group or person? Am I a prisoner of fear, anxiety, worry, guilt, inferiority, or hatred of myself?

## PENITENTIAL RITE (OPTIONAL)

If a group of people are praying in unison, a penitential rite from the *Roman Missal* may be used:

*All:*   I confess to almighty God,
and to you, my brothers and sisters,
that I have sinned through my own fault
in my thoughts and in my words,
in what I have done,
and in what I have failed to do;
and I ask blessed Mary, ever virgin,
all the angels and saints,
and you, my brothers and sisters,
to pray for me to the Lord our God.

*Presider:*   May almighty God have mercy on us,
forgive us our sins,
and bring us to life everlasting.

*All:*          Amen.


HYMN: "BEHOLD, A ROSE"

A hymn is now sung or recited. This traditional hymn was composed in German in the fifteenth century. It is sung to the melody of the familiar "Lo, How a Rose E're Blooming."

Behold, a rose of Judah
From tender branch has sprung,
From Jesse's lineage coming,
As men of old have sung.
It came a flower bright
Amid the cold of winter,
When half spent was the night.

Isaiah has foretold it
In words of promise sure,
And Mary's arms enfold it,
A virgin meek and pure.
Through God's eternal will
She bore for men a savior
At midnight calm and still.


PSALM 40:1–8—THANKSGIVING FOR DELIVERANCE

I waited patiently for the LORD;
    he inclined to me and heard my cry.
He drew me up from the desolate pit,
    out of the miry bog,
    and set my feet upon a rock,

making my steps secure.
He put a new song in my mouth,
    a song of praise to our God.
Many will see and fear,
    and put their trust in the LORD.

Happy are those who make
    the LORD their trust,
who do not turn to the proud,
    to those who go astray after false gods.
You have multiplied, O LORD my God,
    your wondrous deeds and your thoughts towards us;
        none can compare with you.
Were I to proclaim and tell of them,
    they would be more than can be counted.

Sacrifice and offering you do not desire,
    but you have given me an open ear.
Burnt-offering and sin-offering
    you have not required.
Then I said, "Here I am;
    in the scroll of the book it is written of me.
I delight to do your will, O my God;
    your law is within my heart."

RESPONSE

May all who seek after you be glad in the Lord, may those who find your salvation say with continuous praise, "Great is the Lord!"

## SCRIPTURE READING

Read silently or have a presider proclaim the Scripture of the day that is selected.

## RESPONSE

Lord, you who were made obedient unto death, teach us to always do the Father's will, so that, sanctified by the holy obedience that joins us to your sacrifice, we can count on your immense love in times of sorrow.

*Glory to the Father, and to the Son,*
*and to the Holy Spirit:*
*as it was in the beginning, is now,*
*and will be for ever. Amen.*

## SECOND READING

Read silently or have a presider read the words of Saint Benedict for the day selected.

## CANTICLE OF SIMEON

Lord, now you let your servant go in peace;
    your word has been fulfilled:
my own eyes have seen the salvation
    which you have prepared in the sight of every people:
a light to reveal you to the nations
    and the glory of your people Israel.

Glory to the Father, and to the Son,
and to the Holy Spirit:
as it was in the beginning, is now,
and will be for ever. Amen.

## PRAYER

Recite the prayer that follows the excerpt from Saint Benedict
for the day selected.

## BLESSING

Lord, give our bodies restful sleep and let the work we have done
today bear fruit in eternal life. Watch over us as we rest in your
peace. Amen.

## MARIAN ANTIPHON

Hail, holy Queen, mother of mercy,
    our life, our sweetness, and our hope.
To you do we cry,
    poor banished children of Eve.
To you do we send up our sighs,
    mourning and weeping in this vale of tears.
Turn then, most gracious advocate,
    your eyes of mercy toward us,
    and after this exile
    show to us the blessed fruit of your womb, Jesus.
O clement, O loving,
O sweet Virgin Mary. Amen.